THE PICTURE LIFE OF
CORAZON AQUINO

MARGARET M. SCARIANO

D1644035

Franklin Watts | New York | London | Toronto | Sydney | 1987

Cover photograph courtesy of Christopher Morris/Black Star

Photograph courtesy of:
Bettmann Newsphotos: pp. 6, 36, 42 (top), 45, 52, 55
(Reuters), 11, 15, 19, 28, 38, 42 (bottom), 48, 49, 56 (UPI);
AP/Wide World Photos: pp, 12, 26, 31, 61; Picture Group:
pp. 21 (Nik Kleinberg), 32 (Reza/Keystone—Paris).

Library of Congress Cataloging-in-Publication Data

Scariano, Margaret.
The picture life of Corazon Aquino.

Includes index.
Summary: Traces the life of the Philippino leader,
discussing the challenges she faced in her first few
months in office following the defeat of Ferdinand
Marcos in the 1986 election.
1. Aquino, Corazon Cojuangco—Juvenile literature.
2. Philippines—History—1986-   —Juvenile literature. 3. Philippines—Presidents—Juvenile literature.
[1. Aquino, Corazon Conjuangco. 2. Philippines—
Presidents] I. Title.
DS686.616.A65S33 1987   959.9'046'0924 [B] [92] 87-6196
ISBN 0-521-10296-3

CONTENTS

CHAPTER ONE

CORY POWER

February 25, 1986, was one of the strangest days in the history of the Republic of the Philippines. On that day, the nation swore into office *two* presidents. One was a long-time dictator. The other was a woman who was fighting to free the country from the dictator's rule.

Ferdinand Marcos stepped onto the balcony of Malacanang Palace. Before a crowd of four thousand supporters, he took the oath of office. He was sixty-eight years old and had been elected the country's president twenty years earlier. But, on a midnight fourteen years ago, he had become more than the president. Faced with an uprising against his corrupt ways, he had placed the country under martial law (rule by the army) and had declared himself dictator.

In Manila's Club Filipino across town from the presidential palace, fifty-three-year-old Corazon C. Aquino, known throughout the country as Cory, read the oath of office. With her were several hundred friends, relatives, and supporters. In a clear and deter-

mined voice, she told them that Marcos had taken away "the rights and liberties of the Philippine people on that dark midnight fourteen years ago." Now she promised to return those rights and liberties to the people.

As Cory spoke, the sunlight came through a window and shone on her yellow dress. It seemed to echo her hope of a bright new day for the Republic of the Philippines.

Cory and Marcos had just fought a hard battle for the presidency. Both claimed victory at the polls. Marcos, a brilliant lawyer, had years of political experience behind him. Corazon Aquino had never held a political office.

The world had watched their battle with deep interest. It now watched to see which one would finally emerge as the country's president. The United States was watching with particular interest. It had close ties with the Philippines. Those ties dated back ninety

Opposite above: On February 25, 1986, Ferdinand Marcos is sworn in as president of the Philippines. With him is his wife, Imelda. Opposite below: Corazon Aquino, too, is sworn in as president. Supreme Court Justice Claudio Teehankee administers the oath of office. Holding the Bible is Aurora Aquino, Cory's mother-in-law.

years to the time when the United States had fought a war that released the Philippines from four centuries of Spanish rule.

THE SPANISH-AMERICAN WAR

The United States declared war against Spain in 1898, in great part to rid two areas of the world of Spanish rule. The war—known as the Spanish-American War—lasted less than four months. America emerged as the victor. The conflict caused several Spanish possessions to change hands.

In the Caribbean Sea, Cuba was put under U.S. protection until it could form its own government. Puerto Rico was given to the United States. Thousands of miles across the Pacific Ocean, the United States received Guam and the right to purchase the Philippines for $20 million.

Puerto Rico and Guam remain U.S. possessions to this day. The Philippine Islands became an American colony. In time the Islands became an independent country—the Republic of the Philippines.

THE PHILIPPINE ISLANDS

The Republic of the Philippines covers a group of 7,100 mountainous islands off the southeast coast of Asia. Over 55 million people of many different tribes live on these tropical islands. From north to south, the islands stretch 1,100 miles (1,771 km). But if all were pressed together, they would be about the size of Nevada. Ma-

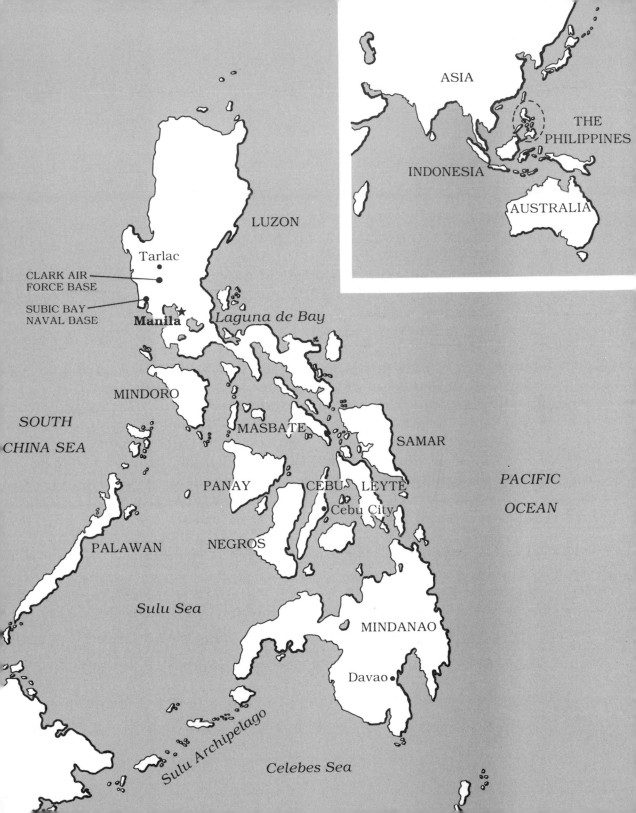

nila, located on the island of Luzon, is the capital of the Republic. Luzon is the largest island in the Philippines.

When the United States purchased the Philippines, it wanted the islands for three reasons. First, the United States was becoming a world power. The Philippines would serve as a fine location to build military bases. Second, the islands would enlarge America's trade interests because they were close to the Orient. Third, some people wanted to bring American civilization to Asia. They did this by constructing roads, forming a government, building schools and sending public school teachers to educate the Filipinos in American ways.

For almost fifty years, the United States governed the Philippines. In 1934, the United States agreed that the Philippines should be an independent country and began a program to help the Filipino people form a government of their own. The program was delayed because of World War II. Finally, in Manila, on July 4, 1946, the American flag was lowered on one pole. On another, the Philippine flag of red, white, and blue, with a golden sun and three stars, was raised. Cory Aquino, who would one day be the country's first woman president, was thirteen years old at the time.

Filipino veterans of the Spanish-American War march in the Independence Day parade in Manila on July 4, 1946.

In front of a large Coca-Cola sign, students and workers in Manila present an "anti-imperialism" skit in 1971, denouncing the "continuing poverty of the masses and the mounting abuses of the administration," accusing the United States and the Marcos government of being the main cause of the worsening economic conditions of the country.

PRESIDENTS OF
THE PHILIPPINES

Until the day years later when Cory became president, the country had six presidents. Five were Manuel M. Roxas, Elpidio Quirino, Ramon Magsaysay, Carlos P. Garcia, and Diosdado Macapagal. Macapagal was elected in 1961. He ran for reelection in 1965, but was defeated by Ferdinand Marcos, a forty-seven-year-old lawyer.

Marcos took office in troubled times. Filipino students protested his support of the United States in the Vietnam war. The crime rate was exceedingly high. When he began his second term in the 1970s, there were economic problems and high unemployment. There was trouble because of tribal and religious differences. On top of all else, there was another problem. Thousands of students, laborers, and farmers were demonstrating because they did not think the Marcos government was treating them fairly.

The most outspoken critic of Marcos's administration was Cory's husband, Benigno S. Aquino, Jr. Benigno and Cory were married in 1954. They became the parents of five children.

Benigno's service to the government began when he was only twenty-two years old. He negotiated the surrender of a rebel leader who had long fought the government. Benigno became mayor of his hometown in the province of Tarlac and later served as governor of his home province. In 1967 he was elected senator and served in the nation's capital. Benigno was considered to be Marcos's major opponent in the next presidential election.

But before the election could be held, demonstrations by students, laborers, and farmers against his corrupt rule gave Marcos the excuse to take action. In 1972, he claimed that the demonstrators were led by communists and "people under the influence of drugs." Some sources believe that some of the violence was arranged by Marcos so that he would have a reason to declare martial law. This action took away freedom of speech and freedom of the press. Marcos dissolved the Congress and cancelled elections. But more importantly, by declaring martial law, Marcos extended his presidency beyond the constitutional limit of eight years. Marcos was now a dictator. He imprisoned the political leaders who opposed him. Cory's husband was arrested and sentenced to solitary confinement.

Nine years later, in a bid to quiet the angry Filipinos, Marcos ended the martial law. Political prisoners were released. Aquino had been freed earlier to undergo surgery in the United States for a serious heart ailment. Marcos was elected to a new term as president in June, 1981.

Soldiers with drawn guns stand beside the body of Benigno Aquino (in white) shortly after he was shot and killed. The other man lying beside him was said to be one of the assassins.

TRAGEDY AT THE
MANILA AIRPORT

After three years in the United States, Benigno—or Ninoy as he was nicknamed—was ready to return home and help free his country from the Marcos dictatorship. Cory was fearful for Ninoy's safety. The Marcos government had warned her husband to stay away from the Philippines. But Ninoy believed that he must help his people at all costs. He told Cory, "I will never forgive myself if I could have done something and I did not do anything." He defied the Marcos warning and set out for the Philippines. Cory and the children were to come later.

On August 21, 1983, Ninoy's plane landed at the Manila International Airport. Although thousands of cheering people waited to welcome Ninoy, they were kept away from his plane by airport security forces. Not even Ninoy's mother and brothers and sisters were allowed to enter the immigration area. A civilian eyewitness on the same China Airlines flight that carried Ninoy home said she saw Benigno Aquino, escorted by a group of soldiers, leave the plane. From the window of the plane she saw a soldier walking behind Aquino on the exit stairway. The man had a gun pointed at the back of Aquino's head. Then she heard the sound of a gunshot. Ninoy fell forward. He lay dead on the ground, a bullet in the back of his head.

Many people were certain that Marcos was behind the murder. Thousands of Aquino supporters jammed the streets. They demanded that Marcos resign. Marcos claimed that he was innocent.

A NEW VOICE
OF OPPOSITION

Corazon Aquino was not on the flight so she didn't see the assassination. But when the killer pulled the trigger and fired the fatal bullet, he unleashed what was to become known as "Cory Power." Her husband's fight for a moral and just government became Cory's fight.

CHAPTER TWO
CORY'S EARLY LIFE

Corazon Cojuangco-Aquino was born January 25, 1933, in Tarlac Province, fifty miles (81 km) north of Manila. She is the sixth of eight children in one of the Philippine's wealthiest landowning families. Only 5 feet 2 (157 cm), Cory may look fragile and in need of care, but in reality she is strong, capable, and fiercely independent. Her dark eyes sparkle with humor or snap with anger at injustice. She is extremely fond of children and children like her. Cory understands the challenges young people face and she is supportive.

Cory grew up on a 15,000-acre (6,000 ha) sugar-cane plantation. Until the Japanese occupation in 1942, Cory's childhood was peaceful and happy. She grew up among a close and loving family with strict rules of conduct. Education and being involved with one's community were stressed. The Cojuangco family had long been associated with politics. Cory's grandfather was a senator and her father was a congressman.

*Japanese troops march through
the city of Manila in 1942.*

Like most Filipinos, she is Roman Catholic. Cory's strength of character comes from her deep religious faith and her strict but loving upbringing.

CORY'S EARLY EDUCATION

Cory attended St. Scholastica, a private elementary school for girls, in Manila. At the end of World War II, she was a freshmen in high school at the Assumption Convent in Manila.

It was at this time that her parents decided to go to the United States. Cory enrolled as a sophomore at the Raven Hill Academy in Philadelphia. Her junior and senior high school years were spent at Notre Dame Convent School in New York. Quiet and shy, Cory missed the Philippines but tried to fit into her new school in the United States.

CORY'S COLLEGE YEARS

In 1949 Cory attended the College of Mt. St. Vincent, which is located in the Bronx in New York City. Her ambition was to become a teacher or translator. Cory speaks Spanish and Japanese as well as English, French, and Tagalog—one of the main languages of the Philippines.

An acquaintance who lived in the same dormitory with Cory remembers her as a quiet girl. She recalls, "Cory was sweet, delicate, and frail. She always seemed to have an inner strength, but she gave no hint of being a leader." But even then, Cory's strong religious faith was apparent. She belonged to Sodality, a college club which studied Roman Catholic liturgy.

Cory's high school yearbook picture.
The inscription below reads, "It is up
to you to bring to the life you are
entering, to the state you must help form,
an energy of true religious faith."

Cory graduated from Mt. St. Vincent in 1953 with a degree in French and mathematics, and was elected to the honor society, Kappa Gamma Pi. This organization is for women in American Catholic Colleges. Top grades as well as moral character are requirements for this honor.

Cory more than qualified on both counts. Her grades were excellent. Although shy, she was respected by her classmates for her concern for others and her strong belief in what she felt was right or wrong. One of her friends said, "Cory's quiet—like a little mouse—until she sees someone treated unjustly. Then she has the courage of a lioness." Her sister-in-law, Nina Aquino, says that one of Cory's strongest traits is her courage.

CHANGE OF PLANS

Returning to the Philippines, Cory enrolled in the College of Law of the Far Eastern University in Manila. There she met Benigno S. Aquino, Jr., an attractive, energetic young politician-journalist, and fell in love. Her study of law soon took second place to her love for Ninoy. On October 11, 1954, they were married in a formal society wedding at Our Lady of Sorrows Church in Pasay City. Cory was twenty-two years old and Ninoy was a year older.

CORY'S NEW LIFE

In the years that followed, Cory and Ninoy had four daughters and one son. While Cory cared for her children, kept house, and was hostess to many gatherings at their home, Ninoy was involved in politics. His first political job was as special assistant under President Ramon Magsaysay. Ninoy's job was to negotiate the surrender of Luis Taruc, the leader of a communist guerrilla force.

After successfully completing the surrender of the communist leader, Ninoy was elected mayor of Concepcion, Tarlac, his hometown. Over the years he progressed from mayor to vice-governor to governor of Tarlac province. His political star shone brightly. In 1967, when he was only thirty-five years old, he was elected a senator. This accomplishment established him as a national figure.

While Ninoy forged ahead in politics, Cory reared their children and stayed out of the public eye. She did not attend political events as many other politicians' wives did. Cory felt that her job was to be wife, mother, listener.

When political groups met at the Aquino home, Cory was a quiet hostess. One of the men present at these political meetings later said of Cory, "She spoke only to ask us what we wanted to eat. She was a good wife, but she made a poor impression." Another said, "She was like a shadow. There, but always in the background."

Cory said that at these gatherings she learned her place as a politician's wife. She would never offer her opinion at the meetings and she would never contradict any of the men. "As far as I was concerned," she said, "I was supposed to just listen. Later, in the privacy of our room Ninoy and I would discuss certain things."

Ninoy was often mentioned as a likely candidate to run against President Marcos in the next election. But before the election could take place, in the dark of night on September 22, 1972, President Marcos declared the Philippines under martial law. This meant that President Marcos and his army had complete control of the government. There would be no elections, no freedom of press or speech. Dictator Marcos dissolved the Congress. He imprisoned thousands of his political enemies.

Marcos said that martial law was necessary because the Philippines was threatened by communist rebels and economic disaster. Many people believe that Marcos's real motive for declaring martial law was to remain in power and get rid of his political enemies.

Ninoy Aquino was one of Marcos's political enemies. When martial law was declared, Ninoy was attending a political meeting at a Manila hotel. Ninoy was seized by Marcos's armed forces and taken to Fort Bonifacio prison. There he was placed in solitary confinement. Almost a year later, he was charged with murder, subversion (aiding or associating with Communists), and illegal possession of firearms.

With Ninoy's imprisonment, Cory's peaceful, private life ended.

CHAPTER THREE

CORY: NINOY'S EYES AND EARS

When Ninoy was sentenced to jail, Cory, in effect, also received a sentence. Now she had to assume complete responsibility for the rearing of their five children. Now, more than ever, she had to make sure her children learned a most important lesson—to love other people. Alone, she had to keep stability in the home. Most importantly, she had to make sure that her husband knew she loved him and supported him.

From 1972 to 1977 Ninoy was tried before a military commission three times. Ninoy refused to cooperate with this commission. He said that the military had no right to judge the case of a civilian. Some of his supporters thought that he should beg for mercy. Ninoy refused. He said, "I would rather die on my feet with honor than live on bended knees in shame." Finally, in 1977, after the third military trial, Ninoy was sentenced to death by a firing squad. Immediately worldwide protest poured into the Philippines. Ninoy's sentence was delayed.

All this time, three times a week, Cory visited her

Ninoy, on a hunger strike, is tried by a military commission in May 1975. On his left is his defense counsel, and on his right is Cory.

husband in the military prison. The family celebrated Christmas Eves together. They slept on thin mattresses on the floor of Ninoy's cell. Later, Cory said, "During the years of incarceration, we had all the time in the world in terms of being together and just pouring our hearts out."

Ninoy's sister, Ditas Aquino Ebner, said, "The prison years were when we [Ninoy's family] started really admiring her [Cory]. She never failed to be there and she lived for her family."

It was during Ninoy's imprisonment that Cory's education in politics began in earnest. Cory, who had always been in the background, now became her husband's partner in politics. Perhaps it was during these bitter years that Cory learned another virtue: patience.

JAILHOUSE POLITICS

Six years after declaring martial law, Marcos, in 1978, permitted the opposing political parties to run in the National Assembly elections. He allowed this because he hoped to quiet the opposition's plea for a democratic government. Although Ninoy was still in prison, he ran for office from his cell. Cory became his campaign manager. She handed out pamphlets that told of her husband's views on public issues. She spoke to various groups. She smuggled out Ninoy's writings and brought him messages from his supporters. She was his link to the outside world. Her efforts pulled the opposition party (Laban) together and helped raise funds for other candidates on the Laban ticket.

A family friend, Heherson Alvarez, said that during this time Cory gained much experience in the handling of difficult situations. The woman who had once been a shadow in Ninoy's public life now became a major force in his bid for election.

Meanwhile, Marcos was campaigning hard. Marcos accused Ninoy of being under the control of the United States. He said that Aquino was backed by foreign powers. Because Marcos's charges were made during a political campaign, Ninoy was given a chance to respond—as long as he did not criticize Marcos.

Ninoy's fiery response to Marcos's accusations on national television ignited the people of Manila. Thousands of people jammed the streets shouting, "Ninoy! Ninoy!" Newspapers said that the people's reaction was a moral victory whether Ninoy's political party won or lost.

A few hours after the polls closed, Marcos announced that his candidates, who included his wife Imelda, won all twenty-one seats in the National Assembly. Apparently nothing had changed. Marcos was still dictator. Ninoy was still in jail, with a death sentence hanging over him. But something had

In 1978, in the first election
in the Philippines in over
five years, Cory casts her vote.
Ninoy, while in prison, ran for
a seat in the National Assembly
on the opposition ticket, Laban.

changed. The imprisonment of Ninoy was no longer a political maneuver. Now, after Ninoy's response to Marcos on television, his imprisonment was a source of embarrassment to the Marcos government. In remembering those years of Ninoy's sentence, Cory says, "Those years prepared me for the greatest tragedy of my life."

RELEASED FOR HUMANITARIAN REASONS

In the spring of 1980, Ninoy suffered a heart attack. Imelda Marcos personally checked over Ninoy's medical records. She even visited him in the prison hospital and reported to her husband on Ninoy's poor health. Marcos decided to release Ninoy for two reasons. First, by sending Ninoy to the United States for heart surgery, Marcos would appear as a caring person. Second, Marcos would be rid of a political enemy.

THE AQUINO FAMILY IN THE UNITED STATES

After Ninoy's successful heart operation at Baylor University Medical Center in Texas, the family moved to Boston, Massachusetts. Ninoy was a Fellow at Harvard University's Center for International Affairs for two years. In 1982 he became a Fellow at the Massachusetts Institute of Technology's Center for International Studies for one year. (A Fellow is a visiting professor of a university or college. He is given a certain amount of money to do special studies.)

*Ninoy, recovering from surgery at
Baylor University Hospital in
Dallas, Texas, is shown here with
Cory and their daughter Maria.*

Cory resumed her role as housewife, mother, and Ninoy's companion. The Aquino family lived in a well-to-do suburb of Boston. Cory enjoyed raising her children, watching television game shows like *The $25,000 Pyramid,* reading novels, and bonsai gardening. She took classes in Chinese cooking. One of Ninoy's favorite dinners was Peking duck. Cory had a special oven just for cooking this delicacy.

While Cory enjoyed being "just a housewife," Ninoy studied and lectured on peaceful ways to change a government from a dictatorship to a democracy. One of the terms of Ninoy's release from prison was that he was not to be involved in politics while in the United States. After three years in America, Ninoy decided that his duty was to the Filipino people. He would not cooperate with Marcos. More and more Ninoy spoke out against the Marcos government. Although Cory never expressed her own political opinion in a gathering, she now sat at Ninoy's side and listened. No longer was she "just a housewife," serving coffee and then disappearing from sight. Having been Ninoy's eyes and ears while he was in prison for seven years and seven months, Cory was interested in the political discussions.

Opposite above: Cory and Ninoy in Boston, building a snowman. Opposite below: The Aquino family together.

FATEFUL DECISION

Through his speeches and writings, Ninoy gathered political support among Filipinos in both the United States and the Philippines. At home Marcos increased the size and influence of the military. The military buildup worried Ninoy because with a large army supporting Marcos it would be more difficult to restore democracy in the Philippines.

In May, 1983, in spite of being warned by the Marcos government not to return, Ninoy made plans for his trip home. Cory was against his going. She said that the three years they had spent in Boston were some of their happiest times together. But Ninoy was determined to return to the Philippines and oppose Marcos in the upcoming election. The night before Ninoy left, Cory cooked him his favorite dinner—Peking duck. It was the last dinner she was to fix for him.

CHAPTER FOUR
CORY'S DECISION

On Sunday, August 21, 1983, Cory's husband was gunned down as he stepped off the plane in Manila. Three days later, Marcos appointed five justices to look into the assassination. That same day, Cory and her family arrived from the United States to arrange for Ninoy's funeral.

Still in shock, Cory was met by hundreds of Aquino supporters. Reporters swarmed around the tearful widow. Overwhelmed by the crowd and the reporters firing questions at her, Cory managed to ask, "Why were only three unarmed men assigned to guard my husband?"

The Filipino people, outraged by the murder, asked, "Who killed Ninoy?" Dry-eyed, Cory led a million mourners through the streets of Manila. Years later, remembering that sad day, Cory said, "After Ninoy died, I really amazed myself."

In the weeks that followed, people asked the same question as Cory—why had Ninoy been so poorly guarded? In October, 1983, the justices investigating

Cory and her son Benigno lead a candlelight procession through Manila, mourning the death of her husband.

Ninoy's murder disbanded with no solution as to his murderer. Another commission was formed.

CORY'S ROLE

In the meantime, the Philippine parliamentary election was set for May, 1984. Cory worked to unify various political groups within the opposition. She convinced most of them to enter the 1984 elections. A third of the parliament seats were won by the opposition, but Marcos still had two-thirds of the seats and the power to appoint a number of additional members. Although the opposition had gained no effective power in the legislature, the one-third victory gave them hope of what could be accomplished by serious effort. With this success Cory grew more self-confident. Ninoy's supporters begged her to challenge Marcos, to run against him, to make the Philippines a democracy again. Cory shook her head. "Come on, stop it," she told her co-workers. "That's not my way. I'm just a housewife."

HONORS FOR CORY

Following the successful election, two U.S. colleges awarded honorary degrees to Cory. Mt. St. Vincent presented her with a Doctor of Humane Letters degree; Stonehill College, near Boston, gave her the degree of Doctor of Humanities.

When she received these degrees, she was no longer the shy, unsure girl of college days. Now she had an air of authority about her. Former teachers and classmates were amazed at the change in her.

The president of Fordham University confers the honorary degree of Doctor of Law on President Corazon Aquino in September 1986.

In accepting the degrees, Cory said, "Faith is not simply a patience which passively suffers until the storm is past. Rather, it is a spirit which bears things—with resignation, yes, but above all with blazing, serene hope."

When asked about her role in the opposition party, Cory told her former teachers and classmates, "After Ninoy died, all I wanted to do was return to my private world." She smiled as if still not believing her popularity. "The Filipinos wouldn't let me go."

A RELUCTANT CORY

Cory returned to the Philippines in time for Marcos's sudden announcement of a presidential election early in 1986. Cory's supporters urged her to run against Marcos. "What do I know about being president?" she asked.

All summer and fall, Cory agonized over whether she should run against Marcos or not. Supporters, friends, and family urged her to do so. Her head pounded with the unsolicited advice she received.

One night she dreamed she went to church and saw a casket. In her dream, she expected to see Ninoy's body in the casket. But, when she looked in, the casket was empty. Cory believed the dream meant that Ninoy's spirit was now in her. Still, she was reluctant. Then 1.2 million Filipinos signed a petition urging her to run. She had to make a decision.

Alone, on November 10, 1985, Cory prayed at Ninoy's grave. She left the cemetery with her decision. If Cory had needed confirmation of her decision, it came almost immediately. A year previously an independent commission had accused a civilian and twenty-five soldiers, including Armed Forces Chief of Staff General Fabian Ver, of conspiring to kill Ninoy. On December 2, 1985, a panel of three Marcos-appointed judges found the accused not guilty. The next day before a crowd of cheering, tearful supporters, Cory declared herself a candidate for the presidency. She repeated the words Ninoy had once spoken: "I would never be able to forgive myself if I could have done something and I did not do anything."

THE ELECTION CAMPAIGN

Cory had to overcome several obstacles. First, she had to convince the voters that she would be capable of running the government. Second, she was a female in a male-dominated society. Third, she had to unite the various groups within the opposition. Fourth, there was every possibility of a dishonest election. Somehow, this had to be guarded against.

With enthusiasm Cory plunged into the campaign and her supporters were just as enthusiastic. Chants of "Cory! Cory! Cory!" filled the streets whenever she spoke. Raising her arm with her index finger and thumb in the shape of an L, the campaign hand-sign for the opposition party Laban (meaning Fight), she looked out into the crowd. Then she spoke. Her voice was high-pitched with little inflection. She spoke with few gestures. Her manner was sincere and unaffected. The audience listened to her.

Cory learned to turn Marcos's attacks on her political inexperience to her advantage. Speaking to a group of Rotarians, a men's service club, she said, "I concede that I cannot match Mr. Marcos when it comes to experience. I admit that I have no experience in cheating, stealing, lying, or assassinating political opponents."

Cory's most embarrassing moment during the campaign came when she introduced the mayor of one town by the name of the mayor of another town.

February 7 drew closer. The very air of the Philippines was charged with excitement and pre-election jitters.

A TAINTED ELECTION

As tallies were posted, the Aquino party accused the Marcos government of vote fraud. They claimed that envelopes containing ballots weren't sealed, making it possible for Marcos supporters to change the vote. Many outlying towns' votes were not included. They accused Marcos of buying votes and scaring people into voting for him. Then Marcos produced tallies showing his victory of 10,807,179 votes to Cory's 9,491,716. The opposition protested the count. Great masses of people were outraged.

The United States had sent delegates to observe the election. The cheating by Marcos supporters shocked them.

PEOPLE POWER

Defeated in the unfair election, Cory did not give up. With steely determination, she launched a nonviolent, civil-disobedience campaign: no taxes would be paid; no workers at banks or businesses. All businesses

identified with the Marcos family or his associates were to be avoided. Marcos was to be denied moral or legal recognition, thus hindering his ability to govern. It would also cause some of his supporters to desert him.

The success of Cory's nonviolent strategy depended upon the people and three other factors: the church, the army, and the United States. Of these three factors, the church's support was the most important.

THE CHURCH'S POWER

A week after the tainted election, the Philippine Catholic bishops met and stated that the election had been fraudulent. Therefore, the bishops said, the people were not obligated to support the Marcos government any longer. They urged the people to oppose the government by all nonviolent means possible. Since 85 percent of the Filipino population is Catholic,

Above: Campaigning for the presidency on the island of Luzon, Cory makes the characteristic hand-sign for the opposition party, Laban: index finger and thumb in the shape of an L. Below: A police officer escorts a suspected ballot-box thief back to the polling station in Manila.

the bishops' remarks carried great authority. Cardinal Jaime Sin, Archbishop of Manila, praised Cory at a mass and warned Marcos not to continue his cheating ways. The Catholic radio network, Radio Veritas, became the unofficial voice of Cory's party.

THE ARMY'S ROLE

The defection of Defense Minister Juan Ponce Enrile and General Fidel Ramos, two of Marcos's high ranking officials, was the turning point in Cory's campaign. They took their stand along with over three hundred men at Camp Aguinaldo and Camp Crame.

From the camp Enrile called Cardinal Sin and pleaded, "Your Eminence, please help us. The president's men are coming to arrest us."

Over the church-owned radio Cardinal Sin asked the people to pour out into the street between the two camps. Nuns, priests, and civilians turned out. Many knelt in the streets and prayed. Marcos sent military units to take control of the camps. When they came upon the people blocking the way, the military refused to fire upon defenseless civilians. Some of the military defected to the rebels and others turned around and left.

Courageous priests, nuns, and civilians block the military from moving on Camp Crame where rebel army leaders took their stand against Marcos.

THE U.S. ROLE

The United States was interested in the outcome of the election for several reasons. First, the United States had nurtured the Philippines from a colony to an independent, democratic nation. Second, the United States has two military bases there—Clark Air Base and Subic Bay Naval Base. Third, the United States did not want a bloody revolution in the islands. To guard against this, the U.S. government warned Marcos that it would not support any action by the Philippine army, using weapons supplied by the United States, against Filipino civilians. In other words, the United States was not willing to support Marcos any further.

In spite of this, Marcos was sworn in as president. Across town Cory took the oath of office, too. The country had two presidents but no government.

Later that day, with much of his military force deserting him, Marcos and his family fled the country. Senator Paul Laxalt, a close friend of President Ronald Reagan, had advised him to step down. The U.S. government offered Marcos shelter in Hawaii, helped to negotiate the terms under which he left, and provided a U.S. air force plane to take him out.

DEMOCRACY WINS

The Philippines, which in the past twenty years had changed from a democracy to a dictatorship, now sought to reinstate the qualities of democracy with liberty and justice for all. Cory, the Philippine's first woman president, was the people's choice for such a government.

CHAPTER FIVE
CORY'S CHALLENGES

President Corazon Aquino faces serious challenges. Her country suffers vast political, economic, and social problems. Because all the branches of government—the executive, the legislative, and the judicial—had been under the control of Dictator Marcos for so long, the entire system has to be made democratic again. Many people in the cities are out of work, and those who have jobs earn less than they did ten years ago. In the countryside people are even worse off. There the Communist party recruits many young men to join its army and to try to take over the country by force.

In spite of these problems, there is a feeling of national pride among many of the Filipinos. The country has a new president who is honest and determined to better the lives of her people.

A TROUBLED ECONOMY

When Cory took office, the economy was in serious trouble. Fifty-five percent of the work force were unem-

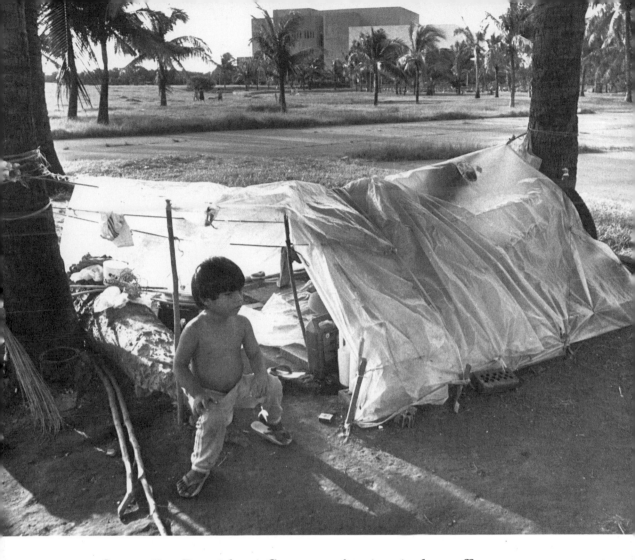

*Opposite: President Corazon Aquino in her office.
Above her is a portrait of herself and
her assassinated husband, Benigno.
Above: On the fringe of Manila, home is a
plastic tent for a child of the Philippines.
Behind him lies the complex where the
International Monetary Fund met in 1976 to chart
the world economic growth for the next decade.*

ployed or underemployed. Inflation was high. Many of the economic problems facing the Aquino government today are a result of what went on during the Marcos era. Many companies are bankrupt and unable to pay back their loans to the government banks, and many of these companies are owned by Marcos's friends who had gotten the loans as political favors.

Since Cory became president, there is more business confidence, but there are still problems that discourage foreign and domestic investments.

Probably the main concern of investors is the government's lack of a firm plan for economic recovery. In fairness to their slow start, the Aquino people did not expect to be running a government and suddenly they were in charge. The new government needed time to decide how it was going to get the economy moving again. In her campaign speeches Cory had said that rural development was an important part of her plans for improving the country's economy. She also pointed out that the country had to increase its exports of goods to other countries in order to pay its bills and earn money to pay for needed imports. The United States and other countries friendly to the Philippines agreed that large amounts of aid were needed. In April and May of 1986, plans for recovery were worked out by task forces and approved by the cabinet in June. The United States transferred the first $200 million in economic aid that same month.

In April, 1986, U.S. Secretary of Defense Caspar Weinberger met with President Aquino. He promised that the United States would put economic aid ahead of military aid in assisting the new administration. Canada, West Germany, Australia, and Japan have also offered assistance.

Later, U.S. Secretary of State George Shultz visited the Philippines. He recognized that the country needed help with its economic recovery. Shultz promised to press other countries to help, too. He also urged American business people to help. The Philippines owe a large amount of money to private American banks. Shultz asked the banks to give the Philippines more time to repay its loans. This would free the Philippines to use its own money for things it needs.

Cory asked her countrymen for their patience in improving the economy. After all, they gave Marcos years to ruin it. Still people were impatient and expected instant solutions from their new president. Cory said, "Look, you were tolerant and so patient under Marcos for twenty years. Here I am only a few days in office and you are expecting miracles. Give me time." Cory hopes to see some economic growth this year—the first in several years.

COMMUNIST
REBELS

Within the first few days of her presidency, Cory freed political prisoners. This was one of her campaign promises. Undoubtedly she remembered her husband's imprisonment for political reasons.

Along with freeing the political prisoners, she proposed a ceasefire between the military and the communist rebels. Cory also offered amnesty (a general pardon) and rehabilitation (retraining) to those rebels who

In the mountains of the central Philippine island of Samar, in 1986, communist rebels come out of their hideout to negotiate peace terms with nuns acting as mediators for the government of Corazon Aquino.

would lay down their guns. Some of them had been fighting the government for over seventeen years.

Critics of Cory's actions said that a ceasefire helped the rebels—by giving them a chance to size up the strength of the government. They felt that Cory was wrong in believing that the communists would cooperate with the government rather than trying to take over themselves. But Cory was committed to giving a ceasefire agreement a chance. She said that if the Communist rebels wouldn't end the fighting, she would, as commander in chief of the armed forces, use the army to end the fighting with force of her own.

MARCOS: GONE BUT NOT FORGOTTEN

The same confidence Cory shows in the ceasefire is present in her dealings with Marcos. Marcos is presently living in Hawaii and Cory wants him to stay there. His supporters have staged rallies in the Philippines on a regular basis ever since Cory assumed the presidency. She says she is not worried about Marcos' loyalists because "when Marcos' money runs out, so will his loyal men."

One thing the new government is concerned about is the supposed millions of dollars Marcos has taken from the government. Cory has established the Commission on Good Government to find Marcos's assets in the Philippines, the United States, and other countries and return them to the Philippine government.

TWO U.S. BASES

For many years the United States has had a treaty with the Philippines which granted military bases at Clark Air Field and Subic Bay Naval Station. Cory has promised to honor this agreement until it expires in 1991. But before she signs any new agreement, Cory announced that she plans to consult other nations in the region and the Filipino people to make certain that leasing the bases is best for her country.

This concerns some Americans, but Defense Secretary Caspar Weinberger said before the House Foreign Affairs Committee, "Let's put our stake in democracy and freedom above the bases." Most statesmen believe the United States is fortunate to have a democratic government in the Philippines again. It shows the world that American political ideas can work in an Asian country. Also, many U.S. statesmen believe that, if the United States helps the Aquino government solve its many problems, the question of the bases will be settled amicably in time.

CORY'S SUCCESSES

Although Cory as president faces many problems, she has had some successes. She restored human rights. She released political prisoners. She has reestablished a free press and removed corrupt officials from office. She has appointed a commission to write a new constitution. Most importantly, she has restored a very high moral tone to the government.

In August, 1986, she traveled to Indonesia—her first trip out of the country since she took office. There

Hundreds of students, wearing papier-mâché masks, demonstrate in front of the U.S. embassy in Manila, protesting the presence of American bases in the country.

*U.S. President Ronald Reagan and Philippine
President Corazon Aquino meet
in the Oval Office on September 17, 1986.*

she met with President Suharto. He announced his support for her and said that he would not back Moslem rebels in the southern Philippines. Filipinos have been concerned that Indonesia, which is 90 percent Moslem, might support the Moslem rebels fighting for independence in the southern Philippines. Recently Cory talked with the southern Philippine Moslem Leader Nur Misuari and agreed to pursue autonomy (self-government) for the 5 million Moslems in that area.

In September, 1986, she traveled to the United States. She had three goals she wanted to accomplish. First, she wanted to establish a friendship with President Reagan and Congress. Second, she wanted to persuade the banks to give the Philippines more lenient terms on its $26.3 billion foreign debt. Third, she wanted to lure American investors to her country. She did establish a personal rapport with President Reagan and her talk before Congress was enthusiastically received. Commercial banks agreed to meet in October to discuss plans to stretch out payment of the Philippines' debt. President Aquino's appearance and personality were key factors in convincing many foreign investors to consider doing business in the Philippines. Cory's visit to the United States was a public relations triumph for her, her country, and her government.

THE NEW PHILIPPINE CONSTITUTION

This document was presented to President Aquino in October. It is an American-style constitution with a U.S. style legislature. The constitution abolishes the death penalty and protects the rights of the unborn. It limits the president to one six-year term and prevents the president from imposing martial law for longer than sixty days without congressional approval. It allows for the retention of U.S. bases in the country beyond 1991. The new document is the first constitution to use the word "love" in its preamble. The public was to ratify this constitution in February, 1987. The election would be a critical test of Cory's popularity.

A RUMORED COUP

In November, 1986, President Aquino traveled to Japan in spite of rumors of a coup (take-over) by Defense Minister Enrile and some of the military. Her trip was successful in opening the way for increased trade between the two countries. She also obtained a $250 million loan for a coal-fired power station. The usually reserved Japanese were captivated by Cory's appearance and they lined the streets shouting "Cory, Cory, Cory!"

One hour after her return to her homeland, news of Rolando Olalia's assassination reached her. Olalia was president of Partido Ng Bayan (PNB) and chairman of Kilusang Mayo Uno (KMU), a militant labor organization with 500,000 members. Both groups are identified with the Communist Party. Members of the two groups accused the military of Olalia's murder in order to sabotage the talks between the government and the Communist National Democratic Front. President Aquino promised that her government would use every resource to bring Olalia's assassins to justice.

TAKING CHARGE

In the months that Cory has been president, she has endured political murders, rumors of a military coup, and criticism for being soft on communism and being indecisive in leadership. Late in November, she took action. She fired her most dangerous critic, Defense Minister Juan Ponce Enrile along with Minister of Natural Resources Ernesto Maceda and Public Works Minsiter Rogaciano Mercado—both under suspicion of stealing government funds. She won a sixty-day cease-fire with communist-led rebels. She told a national television audience, "Of late, my circumspection has been viewed as weakness, and my sincere attempts at reconciliation as indecision. This cannot continue." Her burst of decisiveness and force did not surprise those who know her. A member of her previous cabinet said, "Don't let Cory's gentleness fool you; she's a tough lady."

Cory has matured in the public eye. There is a radiance coupled with confidence about her. She says this is a reflection of the "faith that the Filipino people have in me." Her manner is not the humble one of a year ago. Cory said, "I told Cardinal Sin that I can no longer be humble because people don't take me seriously then, so I have to project my confidence, even more than most men would."

TRAGEDY, DISAPPOINTMENT, AND AN ATTEMPTED COUP

Two weeks before the February 1987 election to ratify the new Philippine Constitution, a pro-land-reform demonstration ended in the killing of twelve people by the Philippine Marines. This was a tragedy and a set-back for Cory's government. At the same time talks between the Aquino government and the communist rebels broke down. Then, just a few days before the scheduled election, rebel soldiers held a television station for two days as part of an attempted coup.

Colonel Canlas, who led the rebellious soldiers, claimed that he and his men were not for or against the Aquino government. He said, "We are fighting communism." But former President Ferdinand Marcos had a 707 jet parked at the Honolulu International Airport, waiting to fly him to the Philippines if the coup were successful. When the Aquino government heard of Marcos's plans, they advised American officials, and Marcos was warned not to leave Hawaii without permission.

Throughout the coup attempt, President Aquino remained calm. She said on national television, "Nothing will derail our effort to establish full constitutional democracy in the coming plebiscite." After several days the rebel soldiers surrendered.

RATIFICATION OF THE CONSTITUTION

On February 2, 1987, the Filipino voters ratified the new Philippine constitution by an overwhelming ma-

*Cory casts her ballot
for a new constitution
for the Philippines.*

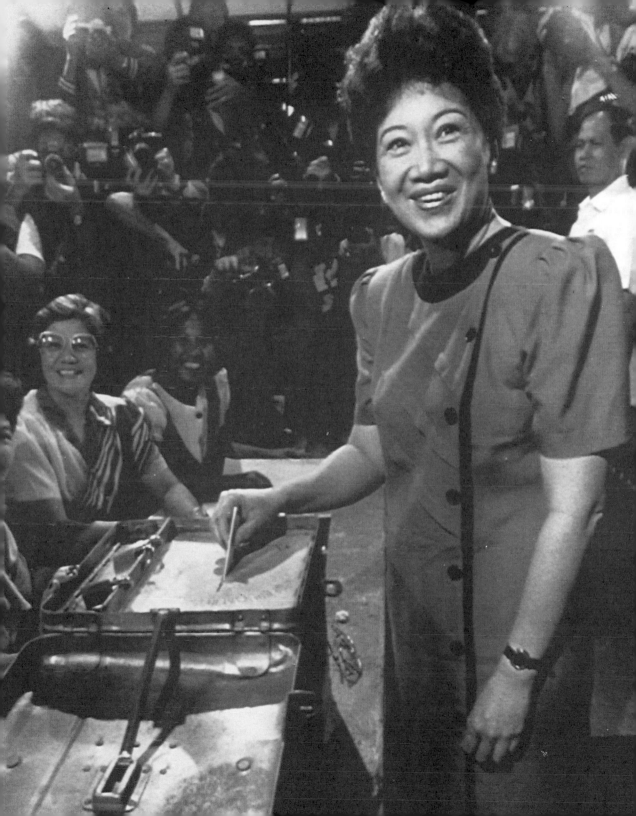

jority and a record-high voter turnout. This victory strengthens the Aquino government's position in handling various problems. Foreign debt negotiations should be eased because the victory at the polls proves that the people support the government. The yes vote on the Aquino constitution disarms her critics. For the communists, who broke off peace talks before the election, the victory demonstrates Cory's popularity. Not only did the constitution win a 76-percent yes vote, but it won in areas nominally controlled by the Communist Party. The communists have several choices now. They can participate in future elections or resume the armed struggle in direct defiance of the people they claim to represent. President Aquino has vowed to continue to seek peaceful negotiations with the Communists but to meet force with force.

And for Cory personally, the yes vote on the constitution was not only a mandate for her government, but an expression of her people's feelings for her. Once again, one year after the first flawed election, Corazon Aquino is her people's choice.

Cory has shown herself to be a woman of contrasting traits. She is small in stature but great in spirit. She is the same unassuming woman she has always been, but she is also a woman fired with faith and courage— a woman who knows herself and the Filipino people. Two years ago she was only Ninoy's widow. Today President Corazon C. Aquino is her people's hope.

INDEX